1 Bristol's well-known apple
woman who held court in the 'nineties
on the corner of Peter Street and
Church Lane, outside Melhuish's
Restaurant; she supplied the dessert
for the lunch customers. A successor
carried on the business until the
Blitz wiped out the seventeenth-
century building

2 *Overleaf* Christmas Steps in the
1900s – the most picturesque
pedestrian way in Bristol; a mixture
of antique and book shops, cafés
and pubs to this day. St John's-on-
the-Walls is now hidden by
Electricity House, but the Corporation
have shown their determination to
preserve the Steps ('steppered down'
in 1669)

FREE HOUSE
CHOICEST WINES & SPIRITS
JIMMY HILLS
GAIETY
A.J. WILLIAMS
PRACTICAL
WATCH MAKER.
WHITE HORSE INN.
H.H. FISHER'S
GENTLEMEN'S HAIR-DRESSING SALOON.
WHITE HORSE INN
VAULTS

Victorian and Edwardian

BRISTOL

from old photographs

Introduction and commentaries by
REECE WINSTONE

B. T. BATSFORD LTD
LONDON

ACKNOWLEDGMENT

All the illustrations are from the 'Reece Winstone Collection of Bristol As It Was'. This was started in 1950, and, at the time of writing, has attained a total exceeding 10,000 subjects; made up of original photographs, negatives, post-cards, lantern slides, stereo pairs, etc. Collecting actively continues; this unique project is to be bequeathed in due course to Bristol City Museum, and the Bristol Archives Department.

Sincere thanks are expressed to those very kind Bristol lovers who have given or loaned material to make so complete a collection – no printed record of comparable value exists for any other English city.

Readers having historical material available for copying are requested to write to Reece Winstone; they are also invited to send any queries on local history to him at 23 Hyland Grove, Bristol 9.

First published 1976
Text copyright © Reece Winstone 1976

ISBN 0 7134 3114 8

Printed in Great Britain by
The Anchor Press, Tiptree, Essex
for the Publishers B. T. Batsford Ltd
4 Fitzhardinge Street, London W1H 0AH

CONTENTS

3 Old Market Street: Mr Pollard's Hat Shop in the 'eighties. No. 83 was demolished in the 1930s, no. 84 in the 1960s, both for road-works

4 The Tramways Centre (*c*.1903), seen from the Brislington–Hotwells tram top (cabs are still horse-drawn). In the left distance the site is cleared in Thunderbolt Street for the erection of the C.W.S. building, opened 16 May 1906

INTRODUCTION

No doubt some readers of the book will be unfamiliar with Bristol landmarks so a few topographical details may be helpful. At the turn of the century 'The Centre' of today began to assume its present importance. Before that time, the natural hub of activity was the site of the High Cross at the meeting of the four streets of medieval Bristol and Saxon 'Brigstowe'. On one of these corners stood the prominent Dutch House (Fig. 7). Bristol Bridge and Old Market Street were secondary centres. Gradually, as the terminus for the electric trams became established in the mid-1890s, the former 'Drawbridge' became 'the Tramways Centre' (Fig. 19), shortened to 'the Centre'. By 1940 the trams had gone, air raid shelters appeared; by 1950 Corporation rockery etc. was substituted and the space between Broad Quay, St Augustine's Parade and Colston Avenue became the Centre Gardens of today – but still simply the Centre in the local idiom.

At the dawn of photography Bristol was of course a very much smaller place, and Clifton was simply a village separated from the town by Brandon Hill. Gradually the two places were linked by roads lined with villas, but the northern boundary stopped at Durdham Down. Then in 1904 came further expansions taking in the north-west village of Westbury-on-Trym and other rural communities to the south and east. By 1910 public transport had extended to include electric trams, motor buses, motor taxis, and the foundation of the Bristol and Colonial Aeroplane Company at Filton (Sir George White being the great driving force in all these enterprises). But in most of these photographs the horse is king.

In 1910 the popular camera of the amateur took $4\frac{1}{4}'' \times 3\frac{1}{4}''$ (quarter plates) photographs, usually on glass plates, although the new idea of cut film in holders was just coming in with the advantage of reduced weight. A dozen plates cost one shilling (5p). The illuminant in the amateur's enlarger was usually a gas mantle – the author used this form until 1934. Tripods were almost always used – 1/25 at F/6.8 was about the norm if your apparatus had a good lens – but 1 second at F/32 was probably more usual, hence wonder is often expressed these days at the splendid detail. Soon there were going to be $3\frac{1}{2}'' \times 2\frac{1}{2}''$ cameras with F/4.5 lenses, and film packs (12 photographs on flat film with a tap to pull after each release of the shutter, taking the exposed film round the back of the pack) but such things were generally unknown in Edward VII's reign. However, the 'small-size' quarter plate was too small for the professional – $5'' \times 4''$ was universal for the press-man even into the late 1930s and the wedding specialist liked a half plate ($6\frac{1}{2}'' \times 4\frac{3}{4}''$) or 1/1 plate ($8\frac{1}{2}'' \times 6\frac{1}{2}''$). These sizes could produce contact prints of sufficient size to satisfy most customers. The commercial and industrial worker would have used $10'' \times 8''$ and $12'' \times 10''$ and there might well have been quite a few $15'' \times 12''$ Victorian cameras surviving. The latter size was ideal a century ago (and even $20'' \times 16''$) before enlarging became universal. Excepting the very adept press photographer, who had to use a hand-held camera, all work was done on the stand. Plates were coated with 'ordinary' or 'orthochromatic' emulsions; 'panchromatic' did not come into general use until just before the First World War. Provided ortho was used in conjunction with a yellow filter, details of cloud formations could be registered in landscape work, otherwise blank skies were the result as we see in Victorian views.

These technical details set the scene for 1910: what of the Victorian decades? George Eastman invented roll film in 1888; Dr Robert Leach Maddox the gelatin emulsion dry plate in 1871; Frederick Scott Archer the collodion wet plate in 1851; and Fox Talbot and Daguerre contributed their own photographic inventions in 1839. Exposures were counted in minutes in the 1840s; there were then no *amateur* photographers: one needed to be both chemist and optician, that is, a scientist with the knowledge necessary to make up one's own solutions, coat one's own plates in the portable tent wheeled to the spot, develop on site with chemicals mixed by oneself, and print the negative on home-made paper. Soon the manufacture of photographic apparatus, plates, chemicals and papers began and things became easier.

In 1853 came the establishment of the (now) Royal Photographic Society and local societies were founded in major towns, spreading interest in the development of the cult. A typical outing is seen in Fig 5. Bristol started its first photographic society in 1866, but already its streets and buildings had been recorded. Fox Talbot himself came from nearby Lacock to take the first photograph of a ship (any ship): this was the S.S. *Great Britain* designed by Isambard Kingdom Brunel (both he and Fox Talbot should surely have received knighthoods at least). This photograph, taken on a paper negative (the 1841 calotype improved Fox Talbot's process), shows the famous vessel being fitted out in 1844, a year after her launching in the presence of Prince Albert. The present work of restoration, which will make her Bristol's greatest magnet for tourists, is being greatly helped by this 130-year-old photograph as it is the only one extant to show the ship before the alterations of later years.

It is not often that the present-day collector of historic photographs can trace the name of the photographer concerned; he can only acknowledge the present owner or source of his find. But now and again the work of a local professional survives in sufficient quantity for his name to be recorded: C. Voss-Bark was active in the 1870s from a studio at 88 Queen's Road, Clifton, alongside the Victoria Rooms – a building later used by Bristol-born William Friese-Greene, inventor of cinematography in 1889.

The York Collection survives in the City Museum: it was said that Mr York photographed every ship that came into Bristol harbour and sold prints to the crew almost as soon as they docked. He was working in the 1890s–1910s.

Fred Little (died 1953) traded from shops in Narrow Wine Street and Castle Mill Street, now redeveloped as one, wide, modern thoroughfare – Newgate; he was well known for a long series of postcards of old Bristol. These survive in their thousands today; Fred Little copied every old view he could find, taking many current views himself, and these are now in the author's collection. The postcard had its heyday in

5　A mystery camera club outing – believed to have been taken in the Bristol district in the 'nineties

the 1900–1914 period when postage was $\frac{1}{2}$d, that is, 42 times less than today, and there were eleven collections on weekdays and two on Sundays.

One of the treasures of the City Museum is a set of 12″ × 10″ paper negatives showing Bristol buildings, taken in the 1850s. These were preserved by the Bristol and West of England Amateur Photographic Association (founded 1866) and presented to the local archives in the 1930s. Their subjects include St Mary Redcliffe before the spire was restored in 1872, the Drawbridge, etc. The Museum Director kindly allowed the author to make prints from these delicate and unique negatives.

The reproduction of photographs in books by the half-tone process was not usual before about 1890. Consequently, a most interesting volume, *A Book About Bristol*, by John Taylor, then City Librarian, published in 1872, was interleaved to allow the pasting-in of real photographs of lantern-slide size ($3\frac{1}{4}$″ square). Strange to relate, the same photographs do not appear in each book; there are variations and it is advisable to examine every copy that comes one's way. The author has traced about ten of these rare books and so copied new discoveries into his collection. It is not yet known whether John Taylor took the photographs himself or employed someone else, but obviously the size of the prints is related to the standard size of lantern slides.

A great newsworthy happening occurred in 1889 when much of the City was flooded by an overflow of the river Froom (Fig 39). A valiant professional photographer, whose premises in Merchant Street were marked by a sign 'Portrait Rooms', set out in a boat and no doubt waded deep in the water to erect his tripod. He produced a splendid set of views, some being taken from upstairs windows. The next editions of the Bristol paper carried some of these illustrations but because the printing of photographs had not become everyday practice drawings had to be made from them and this is the form in which they appeared.

Each decade has its recorder of local landmarks as they change. Those represented in my own collection are:

In the 1900s   W. F. Kuner, C. H. Horton, W. J. Eades, E. C. Stevens

In the 1890s   Edward Brightman, R. W. Coates, W. J. Foster, Frank Holmes, H. C. Leat, J. Nelson

In the 1880s   E. H. Hazell, Arthur Holborn, Mrs F. Wild

In the 1870s   Dr Ormerod, C. P. Lucas, H. Mower

W. H. Barton, active in the 1870s, founded the well-known firm of Harvey Barton Ltd, postcard manufacturers. The famous initials 'G.W.W.' on some of the Bristol views of the 1880s led to their being attributed to the Aberdeen landscape photographer who made it his business to record as many landmarks in Great Britain as possible: George Washington Wilson. A. E. Stanley is remembered with affection; it was to his business that the writer took his first roll of film for developing and printing in 1924. But all the picture research which has given the writer so much pleasure and knowledge, gave him a new career in fact, began in 1940 when the late Mr R. Nutt-Hamblin presented the author with a curiosity – a $3\frac{1}{4}''$ square lantern plate of a view of Park Street taken from the top of a horse-drawn bus and showing another making the climb with extra trace horses attached. It seemed so exciting – a street every Bristolian knows with every building recognisable but the dress and transport so different.

The collector of historic photographs such as these has one recurring problem: how to date and describe the views that he acquires, as in so many cases no information is available. A complete set of street directories is a great help because very often shop-owners' names give a clue, and if half a dozen are visible in one view the span of years can be reduced even more. Old street maps are also useful and the social specialist can use his skill: in what year were such and such female fashions popular? When were motor cars first registered? When did Bristol trams first carry route numbers? When did a certain design of motor charabanc take to the road? For example, a Bristol Blue Taxi with a single painted bead round the bonnet was a Clement Bayard, but if there was a double line it was a Charron. Starting in Bristol in 1908, the cost was 1/- a mile, the driver was paid no wages but kept a quarter of his takings and was paid for the petrol he used. How easy it is to make errors in dating is illustrated in Fig 135: the author assumed the evidence of the ladies' fashions to indicate the late 1890s but when the photograph was examined by a railway historian he was told that the more reliable clue was the station name board on the platform. This standard design was apparently introduced in the year 1904.

Readers frequently recognise their parents in the street scenes; Fig 48 is a case in point – the man in the doorway proved to be the father of two now elderly Bristolians who were delighted to see this photograph. It is strange how some things withstand the

6 Redland Villa, Elm Lane in the 'fifties: an important Bristol family, the Feddens, photographed in their garden. The house survives today as Malvern House, part of Redland College

ravages of time; the marvellous portrait of the Stokes Croft crossing sweeper, taken by an unknown photographer in 1878, was made into a $3\frac{1}{4}''$ square lantern slide and kept no doubt for its novelty. An elderly local amateur, J. A. Basire, gave it to the author some 25 years ago. Other photographs are preserved in family albums such as that of the Fedden family which was the source of Figs 6, 94, and 95.

Most museums now realise the significance and value of old photographs but the layman can still help considerably by holding on to any that come his way. The writer, for example, is deeply conscious of kindnesses extended to him personally; not only do offers of Bristol subjects come in every week, but often packets of postcards etc come through the post anonymously and he is unable even to thank their donors! Perhaps he can take this opportunity to do so.

CENTRAL BRISTOL

7 The Dutch House (1870), the best-known landmark to be lost in the Blitz: 1676 built for a wealthy merchant, 1810 became the Castle Bank, 1826 Stuckey's Bank, 1855 became a shop, 1908 saved from demolition by the Lord Mayor's casting vote in a tie by the Council. It was Mr Tilly, Hatter, who first called it 'The Dutch House' and gave it the fable of being transported here from Holland!

8 College Green, June 1897: the statue of Queen Victoria decorated for the Diamond Jubilee celebrated on 22 June with civic processions, military displays, bonfires, fireworks, the new electric light on the Suspension Bridge, and concerts in all the parks

9 St Augustine's Bridge, looking very new (opened 1893): work proceeds with the lay-out of Colston Avenue (extreme left). The horse bus to Clifton is seen just right of centre. c.1895

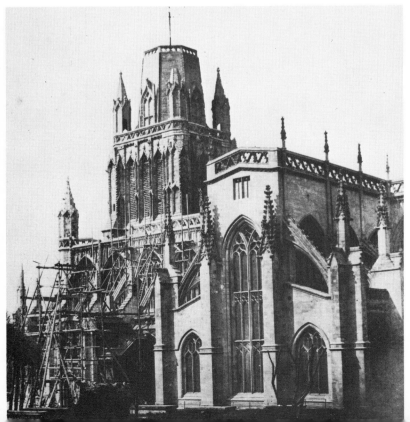

10 St Mary Redcliffe (1858) without its spire, lost in a gale in 1445. A great restoration ensued from 1845, culminating in the new spire of 1872

11 Redcliff Street, 1875: This view, from near Bristol Bridge, shows the improvement when the street was widened from the seven or eight feet in the distance to some 20 feet. By the 1930s trams and increased motor traffic earned it the description 'the most congested street in the country' but Hitler changed all that, and now it has no trams nor any main road significance. Note the new 'Bristol Byzantine' warehouses

12 St Mary Redcliffe Church, c.1872: the view from high up, probably taken during the erection of the spire. Looking towards Temple Meads Station, the goods line is in the fore-ground; the lane left, Pile Street, is now the four-lane arterial road to Temple Way. The pottery cones, left, gave way to factories c.1898; the ground floor of the large one, right, (c.1780) survives as a hotel restaurant

13 St Mary Redcliffe's great frame of scaffolding, when Alderman Proctor Baker, Mayor of Bristol, climbed to the top and laid the capstone, thus completing the 27 years of restoration. 1872

14 Thunderbolt Street in the 'nineties. It was the shortest street in Bristol. This group of houses and shops disappeared for the erection of the 'mammoth' C.W.S. building 1903–1906, which 'little' building was demolished in 1973–4. Extreme left: the Merchants' Hall (blitzed) and next the Merchants' Arms, demolished for the arterial road in the 1930s

15 St Werburgh's Church in Corn Street, removed to Mina Road in 1878. As much as possible of the character of the medieval building was retained, re-erection of the monuments etc. The Georgian houses/shops, right, have long gone – in one of these, it is thought, Chatterton the boy poet was employed in the 1760s. The famous 'Nails' outside the Exchange survive today (tables on the left pavement) – hence the expression 'Pay on the Nail'. Pre 1878

16 Park Street (c.1906), then the most exclusive shopping street in Bristol; the University Tower came at the top of the hill in 1925. The schoolboy playing with a wheel is quite safe – the few, horse-drawn, vehicles do not achieve the speed of modern traffic

17 Bristol Bridge and High Street,
*c.*1895, with statue of Samuel Morley
M.P., the philanthropist (removed to
Haymarket 1921); 'Scholastic' – a
popular shop lost in the Blitz; and
top right St Mary-le-Port church
tower with telephone exchange
gantries

18 Temple Church's leaning tower, in the 'seventies, rises above the 1636 Shakespeare Inn, both safe landmarks still, but the old houses have gone. Temple Church (except the tower) was blitzed and the ruins made safe by the then Ministry of Works

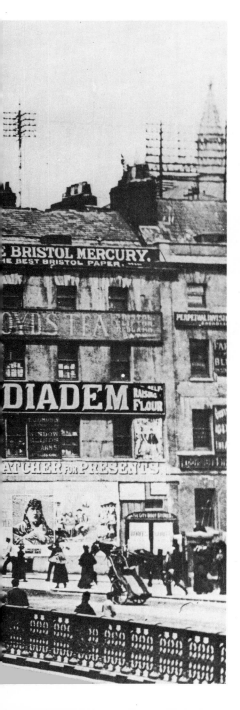

19 The Tramways Centre, *c.*1905, from the tower of St Stephen's Church (already seen in Fig. 9): directly below the three towers of the Cathedral is Smith's furniture shop, the site of Bristol Hippodrome from 1912. Trams were electrified by 1900, but horses for cabs will obtain until 1908

20 St Thomas Street in the 'sixties. Here Mr Neale sold potatoes, displaying his signs in all directions. The alley is Long Row – a medieval street lost by recent development

21 The Horsefair (1866), where today's big stores rose a century later, covering the open space left and replacing the half-timbered houses right. Note Mr Hawkins: carpenter, joiner and undertaker – funerals were then 'undertaken' by craftsmen in wood

22 Pithay (from 'Puithey', a well close), a picturesque street between Wine Street and Fairfax Street – the sixteenth-century houses were replaced by Fry's chocolate factories in 1897. The same street line survives today between the 15-storey office blocks of the 1960s. The date is before 1897

23 Mary-le-Port Street, *c.*1890, looking towards St Peter's Church. Dolphin Street cuts across in the middle distance. The handsome house (no. 35) was demolished in 1904

24 High Street in the 'fifties: the wall of St Nicholas Church left; in 1864 the Druids' Arms (Mutton chops 6d) was demolished to widen St Nicholas Street, and the Angel Inn, further up, fell in the hole. One office block of the 1950s now replaces all these Tudor houses

25 Small Street (looking down) – where the Guildhall replaced the houses in 1868. The newspaper became the *Daily Bristol Times & Mirror* in 1865. Is that the editor in the silk hat? (1865–1868)

26 Clare Street looking up to Corn Street and All Saints' Church, 1893: Upper storeys of near buildings on the right still survive, with new shop fronts below. Practically all else has been rebuilt

VANISHED BRISTOL

27 Dowry Chapel, Hotwell Road: built 1744, demolished 1872 for the erection of St Andrew-the-Less (itself demolished 1963)

28 St Peter's Hospital, 1873, as seen from Peter Street: the most serious loss of all the historic secular buildings destroyed in the Blitz. Built in 1612 by Robert Aldworth, Merchant Venturer and Mayor several times, in 1695 it became the Bristol Mint, then a hospital for the poor, and in this century the Register of Births, Marriages & Deaths. The smaller house to the left of the four gables was built by John Corn *c*.1400

29 East Street, Bedminster: the tobacco factory of W. D. & H. O. Wills covers the site of old cottages demolished *c*.1890. Here we see Mr C. S. Harris in business as a 'Dealer in Marine Stores' (polite name for junk); he used a dog to pull his rag-and-bone-man's barrow. Mrs Harris is at the attic window – as a widow she set up an eating house here, selling pickled cabbage and onions, faggots and peas, and ½d cups of boiled rice. She died in 1919 aged 87. Pre 1890

30 Horsefair in the 'sixties: corner of Lower Union Street off right. Old clothes were sold in these seventeenth-century houses, rebuilt by the 1880s and again in the 1950s

31 Colston Street before 1863. This is now the site of the Colston Hall (The City Hall) completed 1867. Here it is seen as 'The Great House', where Queen Elizabeth stayed for a week in 1574. John Young was then the resident and was knighted by Gloriana for his hospitality. His resplendent tomb is in the Cathedral. The Red Lodge in Park Row (now an Art Gallery activity) is the sole remnant of this splendid sixteenth-century property. Sugar was made here, and then in 1797 Edward Colston purchased the house for £1,300 and adapted it for school use – Colston's Boys' School stayed here until 1861

32 Lewin's Mead before 1878: the Greyhound Tavern was demolished in 1878 for the erection of a brewery. Latimer records that this street was notorious for the degraded character of its inhabitants

33 Cumberland Road Jail in the 'seventies, seen from Coronation Road. Opened 1820; burnt by the rioters in 1831 and rebuilt soon afterwards; closed 1883 in favour of the new prison at Horfield; demolished 1898. Part of the central gateway survives today in ruins; cell blocks are seen either side of the impressive Governor's House. To the left, distant: the Cathedral's western towers are half completed

STREET LIFE

34 High Street (1890–94) from Bristol Bridge: pedestrians use the paved crossing, kept clear of mud by crossing sweepers. St Nicholas Church left; Christ Church in the distance; all shops lost in the Blitz

35 At 2.10 pm on 15 November 1899: A visit from Queen Victoria. The procession comes up from St Augustine's Bridge to College Green, following the public knighting of Herbert Ashman outside the (old) Council House in Corn Street – the Queen's last personal conferment of a knighthood. (Mr Ashman was the first Lord Mayor of Bristol; the office was made a *Lord* Mayoralty in the summer of 1899.) The ships are H.M.S. *Antelope*, the *Menapia* and the dredger *Bulldog*

36 The Kingswood Market Woman, *c*.1870. She came in from the country to sell her produce. (See also Fig 44)

37 *Right* Corn Street (1894). The lady has driven her 'Governess Cart' in from the country

38 *Opposite* St Augustine's Parade, 1906 (compare with Fig. 19). Smith's furniture shop became the Hippodrome in 1912; the Drawbridge Hotel is still a pub, but all else have changed their name boards although the upper storeys show little change otherwise

39 Broadmead, photographed on 9 March 1889, looking towards the Arcade from the corner of Union Street, now entirely replaced by the chain stores of the 1950s/1960s. This was the scene during the most disastrous floods for two hundred years. In the centre, the sign of a star indicates an early music hall, seating 300, named (1874–1880) Alhambra; (1889–1895) New Star; (1896–1900) Tivoli Palace

40 Dolphin Street on 9 July 1908, decorated for the visit of King Edward VII and Queen Alexandra when H.M. opened the Avonmouth Dock bearing his name. This street was totally destroyed in the Blitz and is quite unknown to post-war Bristolians despite it being amidst the city churches. Note the Corporation water cart

41 Queen's Road on 9 July 1908. The royal visitors, having lunched in the City Art Gallery, set off for Avonmouth where the royal yacht *Victoria & Albert* broke the ceremonial tape and so opened the Royal Edward Dock. Around the entrance veterans of the Crimean War and the Indian Mutiny of the 1850s stand guard

42 Hanover Street before 1910 – a narrow way from St Augustine's Parade to Denmark Street, built in 1716. The Georgian houses were demolished to make way for the Bristol Hippodrome, completed 1812

43 The Tramways Centre (then its new name) in 1899: a horse-bus bound for Clifton, its driver protected from the rain, will receive the help of two additional horses for the steep pull up Park Street. Behind are single and double decker horse trams. Thornley's Hat Shop (extreme right) was demolished 1901

44 Clouds Hill Road, St George, in the 'eighties: Mrs Phipps of Cadbury Heath, the 'Kingswood Market Woman' seen in Fig 36, drives past the World's End public house on the corner of Whiteway Road

45   Bristol Bridge to High Street about 1889 (a closer view of Fig 34): a paved crossing kept clean by a crossing-sweeper leads to the Morley statue with its gossipers and the handsome gas lamp by the St Nicholas Fountain (the latter a Blitz casualty)

46   *Opposite* Silver Street – Haymarket corner in the 'nineties. The Round House survives today as a clock and watch shop

47   Redcliff Hill (1906). A shopping street of long ago: Jackson the draper (goods hung outside); Cole the plumber; Collard the butcher; Poole the baker, and the 'Redcliff Blue School and Training Home' run by Miss L. Harris

48 Ellbroad Street in the 1900s (now submerged beneath an eight-lane throughway) when these pigs, unloaded in Bristol Harbour, were on their way to a nearby tannery

49 St Augustine's Parade (1893), looking towards the Exhibition in the new Colston Avenue, just made as a result of covering over the River Froom. Two trace horses return from hauling horse-buses up Park Street. This is six years earlier than Fig 43 and is almost the same spot

50 *Opposite* High Street in 1908: the top of Bristol's first street – a grand hugger-mugger of signs: Carlo Jacomelli's restaurant, Salmon & Gluckstein's tobacco shop, Northam's tea at 1/3d per pound. Only Christ Church looks the same today – all the buildings on the right were lost in the Blitz

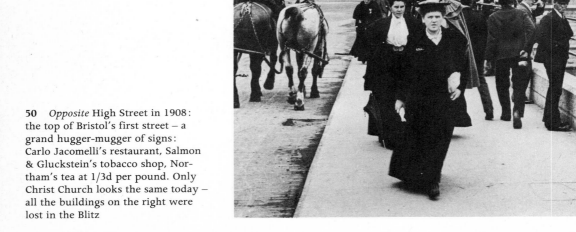

51 Bristol Bridge in the 'eighties: Victoria Street in the distance, with the six-storey Robinson building of 1875. In 1962 it was replaced by the city's first 15-storey office tower. Clogs are worn in the roadway and the woman in the gutter sells her garden produce

52 Baldwin Street (*c*.1860), seen from Bristol Bridge (opposite direction from Fig 51). Market women sell their produce and horse-drawn traffic is glimpsed beyond. In the 1880s the right-hand buildings were demolished and the street much widened. The left-hand side changed slightly and now postwar office blocks dominate the distance

53 The Dutch House, about 1902, thirty years after its appearance in Fig 7. Note the change in trade signs, and in people's dress. The wooden battlement added by Mr Tilly stayed until the reconstruction in 1908

CLIFTON

54 Clifton Suspension Bridge soon after its opening on 8 December 1864 – the handsome lamp standard has since disappeared

55 Clifton Suspension Bridge in the making (1864), taken from the top of the Clifton side tower, looking to Leigh Woods. The chains are in position but the roadway is not yet joined; the chains came from the old Hungerford Bridge in London

56 Clifton Suspension Bridge (1862), Clifton side, with Sion Hill in the background: note the heavy wooden scaffolding, erected when the engineers of Great Britain decided to complete the bridge as a memorial to Isambard Kingdom Brunel. When the two towers had been completed the money had run out in 1843; by 1853 Clifton Improvement Committee was calling them 'follies' and appealing for their demolition

57 *Right* Victoria Rooms (1866) (opposite the R.W.A., Fig 59). Designed by Charles Dyer (1839) for public meetings, balls, etc. Its railing-topped walls were removed when the Edward VII statue was erected in 1912

58 *Below right* Jacob's Wells in the 'seventies: formerly the White Hart Inn, the house is apparently up for sale, and was demolished in 1877. St Peter's Church was here from 1882 to 1939, and now tower flats occupy the site. On the left, the Methodist Church became a library (1888–1905). Between rise White Hart Steps leading to Clifton Wood – still commemorating the old inn today

59 Royal West of England Academy in the 'sixties. Opened in 1858, the original exterior staircase was incorporated inside in the 1912 alterations

60 Sion Hill in the 'fifties. A closer view of the terrace seen in Fig 56 — its Georgian architecture (mainly surviving today) graced by crinolined ladies in the foreground. A hotel of the 1890s fills the space on the extreme right

61   Clifton Parish Church, St Andrews, in the 'sixties. It was completed 1822, blitzed 1940, and its surviving tower demolished (unsympathetically) in 1954. The neat little Georgian dwellings have now given way to industry

SPORT

62 A. E. Johnson, pioneer Bristol motorist (died 1947), with his $1\frac{1}{4}$ h.p. Beeston motor tricycle, the first in Bristol (1896). In 1898 he became head of the Bristol Motor Co., and drove the first motor car from Bristol to London

63 Bristol Camera Club (pre 1903) at the Globe Hotel, Stokes Croft (blitzed 1940). Seated fourth from left: Elwin Neame, whose son Ronald made *The Magic Box* for the 1951 Festival of Britain – the biography of Wm Friese-Greene, Bristol-born inventor in 1889 of the ciné-camera

64 Ashley Down, *c*.1888: the County Ground, where cycle racing was inaugurated in 1888. This may have been the first meeting

65 The Zoological Gardens in the 'nineties, when the bandstand was sometimes used for a trapeze and high-wire act

71 Baldwin Street at 9.30 am on 15 August 1898: ten camels of Barnum & Bailey's circus, the 'Greatest Show on Earth'. To advertise it, the great cavalcade went round the town, finishing at the fairground at Luckwell Lane, Bedminster. Workmen erecting the Scottish Widows' Offices (pulled down 1973) watch the scene; the advertisements include 'Anglo-Bavarian Ale from Shepton Mallet', Variety at the Empire and People's Palace, Cycle races at the County Ground

72 A. E. Johnson at the wheel of a $3\frac{1}{4}$ h.p. Progress car, which drove non-stop from Bristol to Coventry in five hours (1899). The driver's view is impeded by his passengers. In 1902 his firm made the first Bristol car, 10 h.p., 2 cylinder

73 A tricycle built for two in the 'nineties. The male shelters behind the female, who would be the first to suffer in a spill

EDUCATION

74 St George British School in 1895 – 75 children under the gas jets; the notice reads 'Scholars should be regular in attendance, punctual morning and afternoon, obedient to teachers, attentive to lessons, careful in the use of books, kind to one another'. Opened in 1853, it moved in 1900 to newly erected Summerhill School, and the old buildings became a Baptist Church

75 The Blue Maids' Orphanage, Ashley Hill, in the 'nineties. It was founded in Ashley Manor House in 1795, with accommodation for 50 orphans but funds for only 15. However, money came in and by 1829 this building was erected where 60 orphans lived. In 1911 the original seventeenth-century house was demolished and in 1927 the Orphanage closed

76 The Red Maids' School, Denmark Street, in the 'seventies. It was endowed by Ald. Whitson in 1627 for the 'clothing, educating and maintenance' of 40 girls. This building, Gaunts' House, adjacent to St Mark's, College Green, was the home of the school from 1843 to 1911 when modern buildings were erected at Westbury-on-Trym

77 Redcliffe School Band (1885) Mr J. T. Francombe, on the left, taught his boys music and swimming, extremely rare school activities then. 'Francombe of Redcliffe' (1844–1924) was Lord Mayor 1919–20

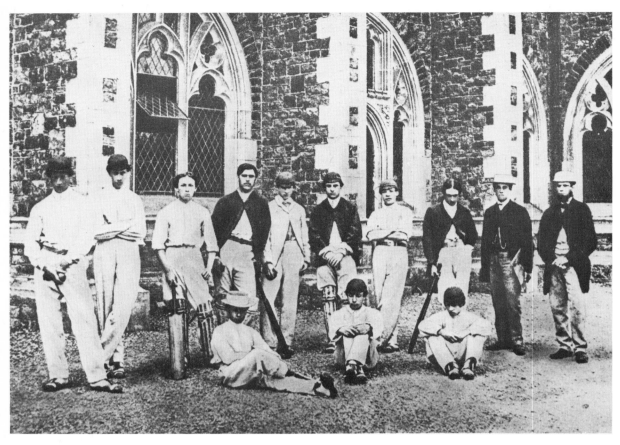

78 *Top left* Clifton College: the cricket eleven of 1864, two years after the famous public school was founded

79 *Left* Clifton College: the masters pose for the camera in 1865; the seated figure is no doubt the Head

80 *Above* Cricket on the Downs in 1867. The adult was James Chard (born 1845), a master of the Anglesea Place School, Worrall Road, nearby

MIDDLE CLASS

81 Rupert House: the garden in the 'sixties   **82** Rupert House: tea on the lawn in the 'sixties

83 Rupert House, St Michael's Hill (early 'sixties): a seventeenth-century house near the church, named after the occasion when Prince Rupert hid nearby during the Civil War. With the making of Perry Road in 1871, the fine views over the city from its garden were lost, and later the house itself disappeared

84 *Below* Rupert House: an interior view in the 'sixties

85 Clifton in the 'sixties: Church Walk, connecting St Andrew's, Clifton Parish Church, to Victoria Square. This avenue is now the famous example of 'pleached' limes. The church has now gone

86 *Below* Clifton in the early 'seventies: on the extreme left is Christ Church (the parish church following the blitz of St Andrew's). The Georgian house next to it was known as 'Urch Cottage'; William Friese-Greene had his first photographic darkroom here, by permission of his aunt, Jessie Carter

OCCUPATIONS

87   The Wash-tub: an illustration of the 'fifties from the Fedden family album

88   Westbury-on-Trym (1895): Water Lane (formerly Betty Waters Lane), where Mr Radford,
Smith, serviced the then village (not brought into Bristol until the new century)

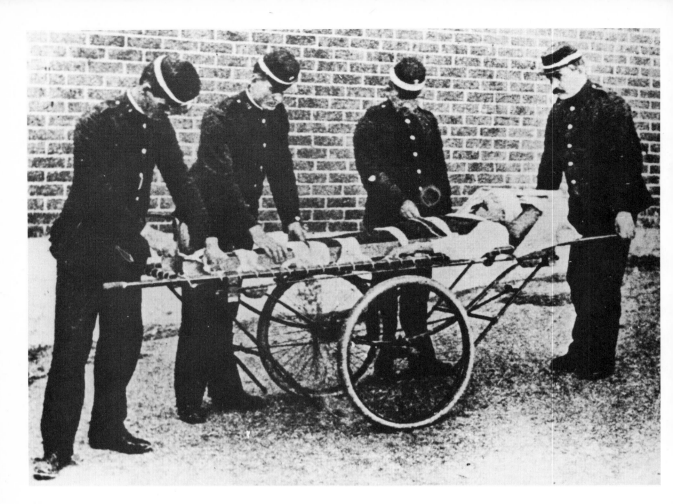

89 St John's Ambulance Service, which began 1887–8, photographed in the 'nineties. This 'Ashford Hand Litter' came in the 1890s; it had folding supports for standing and the stretcher was detachable for carrying. It is still available for use on the Downs

90 Miss Hughes, on duty in the National Telephone Exchange soon after it was opened (1894) in High Street and Mary-le-Port Street. It could accommodate 1,200 subscribers

91 Castle Street, here photographed in the 'seventies, was built on the site of the Castle when Cromwell demolished it. At this date many of the seventeenth- and eighteenth-century houses still survived. By 1939 all had been rebuilt for a conglomeration of chain stores, and it became the busiest shopping street in Bristol. 1940 saw its complete destruction

92 66 Bedminster Parade (1889):
Mr Woodhall the butcher died 1909;
his daughter (on right) became Mrs
Collard, of a well-known firm of local
butchers

HATS & UMBRELLAS

WINSTONES
1 11
Special Value

WINSTONES
26
Special Value

WINSTONES
26
Special Value

J. E. WINSTONE.

93 *Left* 29 East Street as it was on 2 April 1906

94 Two roadmen in Redland (1854) Another study from the Fedden album – the wall and gutter are still there in Elm Lane!

95 Redland Lane (1854), now Hampton Road. The buildings survive: right, 6 Layton Villas; left, 130 Hampton Road. The two-storey barn has given way to a Meeting House of the Society of Friends. Another view from the Fedden album

96 Small Street in the 'sixties: the Great Hall (fifteenth-century), where it is thought Edward Colston's father feasted Charles I in 1643. An extra floor was added and it was used as a composing room for the *Times & Mirror*, then printed here

97 St Mary Redcliffe (1872): the men who built the spire, which replaced the original one destroyed in a storm in 1445. The top hatted figure is probably George Godwin, designer of the spire

98 Dean Lane Colliery in the 'seventies. It is now the site of the Dame Emily Park. The Bedminster coal carts are lined up to collect supplies direct from the pithead

SUBURBS

99 East Street, Bedminster in the 'seventies: 100 yards from the London Inn, the alley was then Georges' Barton, now Church Road

100 Henbury Hill view of Westbury-on-Trym in the 'eighties. The Falcondale Road by-pass was cut across the middle distance in the 1930s, and houses now cover all possible open spaces

101 Bedminster: view from the London Inn into East Street, 1909. The man in the centre (under the word 'Mustard') holds up a notice on a leg, like school wardens today; a white ring meant 'stop', a black ring on white 'go', thus giving long-distance signals to tram drivers on single tracks

102 *Left* Henleaze in 1875, before it became the fashionable suburb of the 1920s/1930s: this picturesque thatched house survives today as 166 Henleaze Road, but here it is seen as the Lodge to Henleaze Park, the residence of the Derham family, which later became St Margaret's School (demolished 1962)

103 *Below left* Hotwells (1867): Rownham Ferry in its original position (where it had been since the Norman Conquest) before removal upstream in 1873, when the entrance to Brunel's Cumberland Basin was changed. The ferry ended in 1932

104 *Below* St George: Croft End Road in the 'seventies: harvesting for all ages in 'Benny Freke's Field' before the houses came in the twentieth century

105 Arno's Vale (1866): the newly opened 'Bristol Cemetery', better known today as Arno's Vale Cemetery. The bare hillside is now completely covered by monuments

106 *Top right* Henbury Hill in the 'seventies, looking towards Westbury (a place much older than big Bristol, which has reached out and enveloped the old village). Now houses and a by-pass cover all the distant empty spaces, but the wall (extreme right) survives

107 *Right* Blaise Hamlet (1866). This property at Henbury has been owned by the National Trust since 1943: a charming group of cottages round a green, with a sundial/fountain, designed by John Nash in 1809 for John Harford's workpeople. Today the cottage interiors have been modernised, but this scene is unchanged

108 Westbury Park in the 'seventies: 'Redland Knoll' on the north corner of Blenheim Road and the Glen. This fine house survives, but the garden was reduced for road widening

109 *Below left* Cheltenham Road early this century. A cinema came midway on the left, named in succession: Cheltenham Road Picture House, the Plaza, and The Academy (closed 1955)

110 *Below* Fishponds tram terminus, *c.*1906 – then the end of the line, which was later extended a mile or so to Staple Hill

CHARACTERS

111   On 18 September 1896 a mentally deranged man from Birmingham threw his children, Ruby (12) and Elsie (3) down into the Avon Gorge from the Suspension Bridge. They landed in the mud and were rescued by James Hazell, pilot, and P.C.s Toogood, Wise and Baker

112   Dr Doudney's Soup Kitchen in the 'seventies. This was established by the vicar of St Luke's, York Road, Bedminster, in William Street when he found he was surrounded by starving and unemployed people. He is seen on the left

113 Samuel Jackson and Francis Danby, both notable painters, photographed in the 'fifties. Jackson (1794–1869) was born in Wine Street, lived at 8 Canynge Square, and died in Clifton. Danby (1793–1861) was elected A.R.A.

114 *Above* Mr William Horwood
(1772–1864), photographed about
1860. He was the oldest Bristol
Volunteer, serving 1797–1814

115 *Above, right* Samuel Plimsoll,
'the sailor's friend', photographed in
the 'seventies. He was born at
9 Colston Parade, 1824; became M.P.
1868, and established his 'Plimsoll
Mark', to prevent the overloading of
ships

116 Mrs Mary Jones, aged 93, in
1884: her husband was the butler to
the Bishop of Bristol at the time of
the 1831 Riots; he saved his lordship's
life when the Palace was burnt down

117 Dr David Doudney (1811–1893), vicar of St Luke's 1859–91, in a photograph of the 'seventies. He did good work in saving starving children. He was also of a literary bent, writing popular religious books

118 Joseph Croot, last Town Crier of Bristol, photographed in the 'nineties. His office came to an end in 1891; he wore a black livery coat with brass buttons, tricorn hat, blue velvet breeches and gaiters, and a huge bunch of flowers

119 Stokes Croft crossing sweeper (1878), taken in a photographer's (daylight-lit) studio

TRANSPORT

120   The Hanham tram (*c.*1900). The design features of early electric trams changed somewhat in later years: this vehicle shows a painted destination board instead of a roller blind box, larger figures than later, unfamiliar caps for the staff

121   Gloucester Road from Zetland Road junction early in the present century: a cab shelter and the B.T.C.C. garage, long gardens and trees in front of the distant houses. Compared with Fig 120, the roller blind box for destinations has been fitted on the trams

122 The Tram Strike of 1901: Brislington Depot furnished with beds for the staff who refused to join their fellows on strike during a dispute. Each man received a silver medal and a bonus: 2/- per week senior staff, 1/- for drivers, 6d for conductors

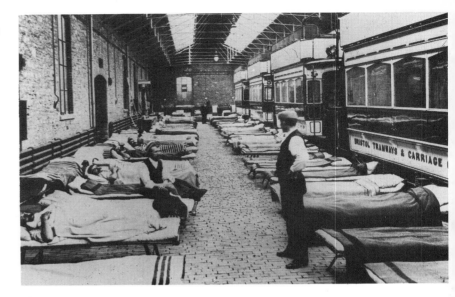

123 Two cyclists on the Tramways Centre, c.1908. Some of the buildings on the right have received new frontages since

124   The first day of electric trams (14 October 1895): Tram 'H' on its arrival at Kingswood from Old Market; the silk hatted figure beside the driver is (Sir) George White (Bart), then secretary, later chairman of B.T.C.C., future founder of the Bristol Aeroplane Co..

125 When, in March 1894, this passenger wished to use the Gas Works' Ferry (Cumberland Road–Anchor Road) it took five oarsmen to overcome the ice

126 *Right* The Tramways Centre B.T.C.C. offices (April 1911). The two vehicles on hire are 30 h.p. C.G.Vs: touring car with cape hood, and the Victoria

127 *Right, below* A steam tram (1880–81): the first effort to mechanise the horse-drawn trams. Its exhaust fumes were carried up and over a fragile roof on the upper deck to save passengers from their effects. The experiment lasted only a year – not surprisingly it caused horses to bolt

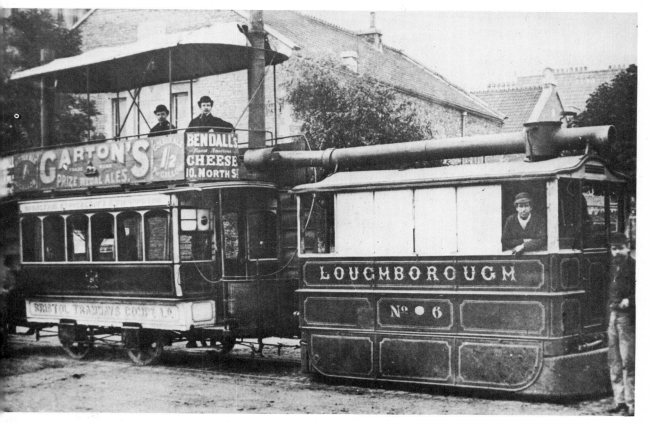

128 *Top left* The first tram (1875): starting from Upper Maudlin Street, and via Queen's Road and Whiteladies Road to the foot of Blackboy Hill (which was too steep for horses). On the front step the silk hatted figure is George White (also seen in Fig 124)

129 *Left* Deanery Road (1899). Cabs beside the Cathedral and raised College Green await custom, offering a choice of open or closed four wheelers, and hansoms

130 Almondsbury bus (1893). This appears to be a private effort (not B.T.C.C.) connecting to Patchway and Filton, and has room for a dozen or so inside and six outside. The background is probably Almondsbury Hospital

131 Electric tram on the Tramways Centre about 1900. In 1900 all tram routes were electrified and in 1902 Thornley's Hat Shop was demolished

132 Westbury to Redland bus
(*c*.1908). This service began early in
1908. It had been two years earlier
that B.T.C.C. motor buses replaced
horse-drawn types from Victoria
Rooms to Clifton Suspension Bridge

133 The car (1902) that received the first registration number (AE1) in Bristol in 1903. It was a Clement-Talbot, 12 h.p., 4 cylinder and capable of 30 mph, owned by Thomas Butler, a local company owner. William Brock was the chauffeur

134 Hotwells horse tram (1880s). The one-penny fare covered 'Joint Station' (Temple Meads) to 'Suspension Bridge' (actually underneath it)

135 Ashley Hill Station. *c*.1903 was the date of this design of station name boards

136 Bristol Box Kite (*c.*1911), the earliest aircraft made by Bristol Aeroplane Co, which first flew in June 1910, with a 50 h.p. engine

137 *Above* Park Street trace horses (1895). Two horses are being added to the normal pair to haul the bus up the steep hill

138 *Top right* The 'Port and Pier Railway' at Hotwells (correctly 'Bristol Port Railway and Pier') in the 'nineties. It was opened on 6 March 1895 and ran along the riverside to Avonmouth until the Portway road was built in the 1920s

139 *Right* Bristol's first charabanc outing, 1898. Mr A. E. Johnson (also seen in Figs 62, 72) drives the Daimler on the left, wearing a yachting cap. Organised by the Bristol Motor Co, the vehicles feature solid tyres, water tanks at the rear (which frequently boiled), tube ignition, and lighting by candles in carriage lamps. The Daimler was 4 h.p. and could do 14 mph, stop in 10 feet, and cost three farthings per mile to run

SHIPS & SHIPPING

140 St Augustine's Parade: looking through the tall masts to St Stephen's Church, 1880s

141 Prince Street Bridge (1856) seen from Canon's Marsh with St Mary Redcliffe (minus spire) on the right. Then merely a footbridge, it was improved into today's inadequate structure in 1879. The tolls on the footbridge were let for £1,100 per annum

142 The 1827 Drawbridge (*c*.1855), on the right, replaced in 1868 by the last and improved bridge (actually a swing bridge). The two churches are the only survivals today: St Mary left, St Stephen right; the further water was covered over in 1892, the nearer in 1938

143 Broad Quay and St Augustine's Parade (right and left, *c*.1871), where some of the buildings survive. The ships on the water have been replaced by motor traffic swirling round municipal rockery

144 Broad Quay (1860–68). A cab stand is at the entrance to the present Canon's Road, the little tower once carried signals to give the all-clear for the ships to leave harbour, then was converted to a 'Gents'

145 *Top* Welsh Back, seen from Bristol Bridge, where ships from Welsh coast ports tied up (1896–99).
The Phoenix, on the far right, called here between the dates quoted. Note the 'Bristol Byzantine'
style buildings on the quayside, lost in the Blitz

146 *Above* Welsh Back, looking towards Bristol Bridge. Cobbles, wagons, tall hats and sailing ships
are the foreground to the three city churches surviving today. Warehouses now stand on the edge of
the Quay. 1860s

147 The Mardyke in the 'sixties. Clifton Wood rises over Hotwell Road and this handsome full-rigged ship from America. Alongside the ship is a 'Gadget': the origin of the now familiar word thought up by a Bristol stevedore, being a barge with a donkey-engine supplying power for lifting tackle on a sailing ship

148 *Above* The S.S. *Gipsy* was wrecked in the Avon Gorge (12 May 1878), striking the bank opposite the Gully. 200 lb of dynamite was used in the clearance operations, and good money was made by brake and cab men taking people to the scene

149 *Top left. Mary Ann Peters* on 14 March 1857, a Bristol barque of 610 tons which became stranded on the mud at Rownham Ferry, where a small crowd is seen on the ferry slip. This little ship regularly carried passengers from Bristol to Quebec

150 *Above. Mary Ann Peters* waiting, on 31 March 1857, for the Spring tide to free her from the mud – a first class illustration of why the bottoms of ships had to be specially strengthened when visiting Bristol Harbour; they had to be 'Ship Shape & Bristol Fashion'. The riverside buildings were swept away in the 1873 extensions to Cumberland Basin.

151 Hotwells (1872–73). The tug is the *Fearless*; work is in progress on the right for the enlargement of Cumberland Basin

152 Redcliff Parade to the Grove (1869–78). On the right of the Sailors' Home, the little pub with a handsome porch, The Hole in the Wall, is the only survival of the quayside buildings. Distant right is the 1869 Byzantine Granary – the most important Victorian composition in Bristol